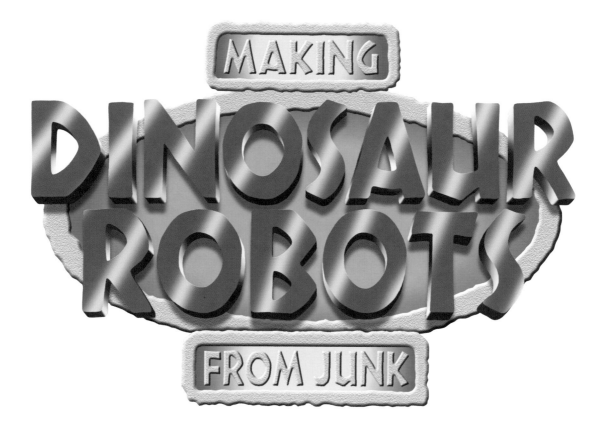

MAKING

DINOSAUR ROBOTS

FROM JUNK

MAKING DINOSAUR ROBOTS FROM JUNK

> HOWDY THERE, I'M MEGA-DON, DINO BUILDER, NUMBER ONE, THERE'S ONLY ONE THING TURNS ME ON, THAT'S BATTLING DINOBOTS FOR FUN!

Sixty-five million years ago the last of the terrible lizard dinosaurs died out. Now they're back and this time they're mean, magnificent and metallic! It's the dawn of the Dinobot Dynasty.

Meet Mega-Don (Dinosaurus Maximus), an expert in robotic dinosaur construction. His trusty assistant, Terror-Ron (Pterosaurus Minimus), sorts through junk. There are five Jurassic junk monsters for you to construct. Each one can be armed with deadly weapons and jaw-proof armour-plating for ferocious dinobot battling.

There are easy-to-follow instructions for all five dinobots, plus hints on using tools, painting and customising your creations. Then check out the stick-tastic sheet of special designs that Don has dreamt up for you. For advanced robot builders there are details on how to electrify each robot with battery power, lights and sound effects.

Whether you wire them up or not, find out all about Dinobot battling in the Battle Bank section. There are ideas for setting up skirmishes and duels, plus rules of conflict and instructions for building a deadly Arena of Extinction in which the weakest link always loses!

> I'M TERROR-RON, HIS TRUSTY FRIEND, I OFTEN DRIVE HIM ROUND THE BEND, COLLECTING JUNK IS WHAT I DO, SO HAVE A GO, RECYCLE TOO,

PARTS DEPARTMENT Once Ron has checked out all the best types of junk, he lists his choice in this section for each dinobot. But remember, this is only a guide. You may find slightly different or better items, depending on where your family shops.

TOOL CHEST You only need a few simple tools for these projects. They are listed here plus tips on how to use them correctly

ASSEMBLY BREAKDOWN Putting a dinobot together is a lot easier than reconstructing dinosaur skeletons from old bones. Just follow the step by step instructions and you can't go wrong.

HAZARD WARNING Don't be a Dip-lodocus. Be sure to read the warnings in this section before you start, and stay safe.

TOP TIPS Don shares his expert knowledge of junk construction with you here, to help you stay ahead of the herd and gain skills and techniques that guarantee great results.

FINISHING OFF Find tips here for finishing dinobots with a coat of paint, special effects and sticker locations for each one.

ELECTRA EXTRA Add a zap of real electro-energy to bring your robots to life. There are instructions here on how to wire them up with motors, lights and sounds, and an integrated remote control unit for co-ordinating your attack from a distance.

MAKING DINOSAUR ROBOTS FROM JUNK

CONTENTS

ADULT HELP RECOMMENDED

Wherever you see this sign, there will be tasks which require the help of an adult. It may mean you need to ask permission before helping yourself to things around the home. Sometimes you may be required to use tools that could be dangerous if you have never used them before. Remember the age-old rule from the dawn of time: Always ask before you do, adults have their uses, too.

PARTS DEPARTMENT

Start looking around at all the amazing shapes that plastic containers and other oddments come in. You'll soon see there are ready-made robot components to be dug up all around the home. It just takes a bit of imagination and a tube of strong glue to turn them into an exciting dinosaur robot or a terrifying Tyrannosaurus. Ask others to start collecting for you as well. In no time you will have everything that you need to make the five projects in this book and a whole lot more.

⚠ HAZARD

- ALWAYS CHECK HAZARD WARNING PANELS BEFORE STARTING ANY PROJECTS. IF YOU ARE UNSURE ABOUT ANYTHING, ASK AN ADULT.
- NEVER USE BOTTLES THAT CONTAIN, OR HAVE CONTAINED, DANGEROUS SUBSTANCES SUCH AS BLEACH, WEED-KILLER OR MEDICINES. IF A CONTAINER DOESN'T HAVE A LABEL, ASK AN ADULT OR JUST DON'T USE IT.
- DON'T TRY SCRATCHING LABELS OFF WITH A SHARP INSTRUMENT SUCH AS A KNIFE. IT MAY SLIP AND HURT YOU. MOST LABELS WILL PEEL OFF EVENTUALLY IF LEFT TO SOAK IN WARM WATER.

Aerosol lids (one smaller than the other so one fits inside the other)

Trigger-action spray bottle

Toilet cleaner bottle with angled neck

Duck toilet cleaner bottle

Lid from a fabric softener bottle

Metal bolts

Deodorant stick container

Large screw-top lids

Plastic jar lids

Pop-up bottle top

Plastic carrier bag

THERE'S SO MUCH JUNK, WE THROW AWAY, AND PLASTIC PARTS JUST WON'T DECAY. SO USING THINGS A SECOND TIME WILL HELP TO BEAT THIS NASTY CRIME.

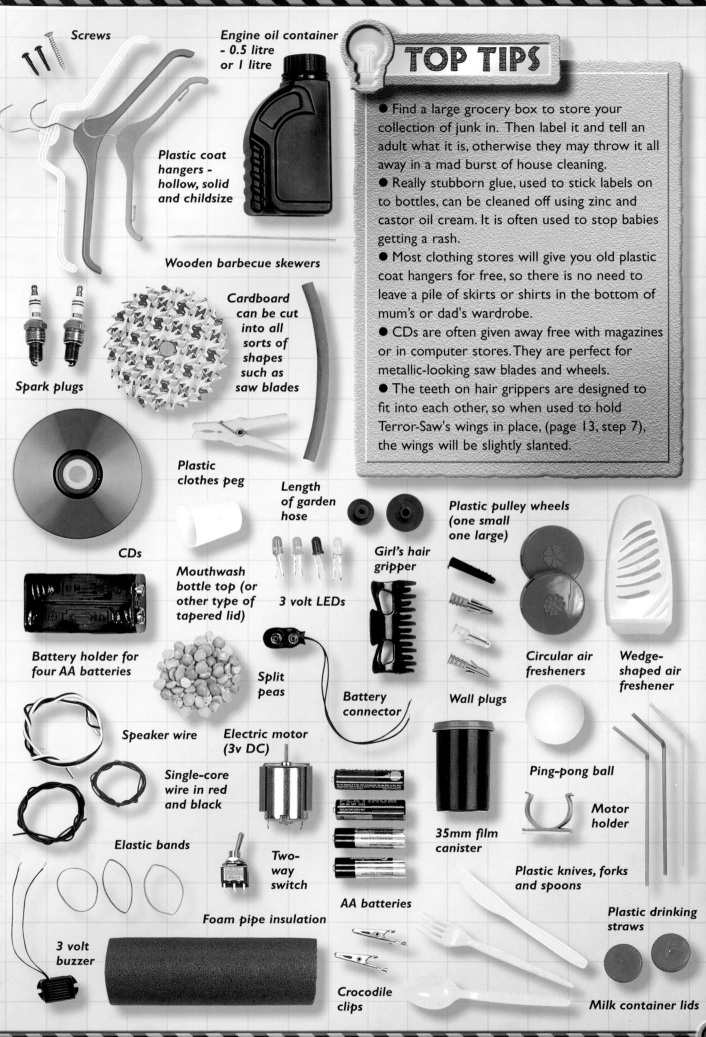

Screws

Engine oil container
- 0.5 litre
or I litre

Plastic coat
hangers -
hollow, solid
and childsize

Wooden barbecue skewers

Cardboard
can be cut
into all
sorts of
shapes
such as
saw blades

Spark plugs

CDs

Plastic
clothes peg

Length
of garden
hose

Plastic pulley wheels
(one small
one large)

Girl's hair
gripper

Mouthwash
bottle top (or
other type of
tapered lid)

3 volt LEDs

Battery holder for
four AA batteries

Split
peas

Battery
connector

Wall plugs

Circular air
fresheners

Wedge-
shaped air
freshener

Speaker wire

Electric motor
(3v DC)

Ping-pong ball

Single-core
wire in red
and black

Motor
holder

Elastic bands

Two-
way
switch

35mm film
canister

Plastic knives, forks
and spoons

3 volt
buzzer

Foam pipe insulation

AA batteries

Plastic drinking
straws

Crocodile
clips

Milk container lids

TOP TIPS

● Find a large grocery box to store your collection of junk in. Then label it and tell an adult what it is, otherwise they may throw it all away in a mad burst of house cleaning.

● Really stubborn glue, used to stick labels on to bottles, can be cleaned off using zinc and castor oil cream. It is often used to stop babies getting a rash.

● Most clothing stores will give you old plastic coat hangers for free, so there is no need to leave a pile of skirts or shirts in the bottom of mum's or dad's wardrobe.

● CDs are often given away free with magazines or in computer stores. They are perfect for metallic-looking saw blades and wheels.

● The teeth on hair grippers are designed to fit into each other, so when used to hold Terror-Saw's wings in place, (page 13, step 7), the wings will be slightly slanted.

TOOL TIME

Melting, cutting, gluing and spraying are the four main tasks you will have to master for the projects in *Making Dinobots*. This means having the correct tools and being able to use them safely and effectively. Find a strong box and collect all your tools before you begin. Find a suitable place to work. A workbench in the garage is best, but a protected table will do. Ask permission and advice before you begin and check out the hazard warnings for each dinobot.

⚠ HAZARD

- BE CAREFUL WHEN USING HEATED BRADAWLS AND SCREWDRIVERS. DIP THEM IN A JAR OF COLD WATER AFTER USE TO COOL THEM DOWN.
- FUMES FROM STRONG CONTACT ADHESIVES CAN BE DANGEROUS. WEAR A PAINT MASK AND ALWAYS WORK IN A WELL-VENTILATED ROOM.
- KEEP GLUE AWAY FROM YOUR EYES.
- PROTECT YOURSELF FROM PAINT FUMES. WEAR A PAINT MASK.
- GET AN ADULT TO FIT NEW SAW AND CRAFT KNIFE BLADES FOR YOU.
- NEVER CUT TOWARDS YOUR HANDS WITH A KNIFE OR SAW.
- DON'T PRESS TOO HARD WHEN CUTTING WITH A KNIFE. IF YOU DO, YOUR HAND IS MORE LIKELY TO SLIP!
- ALWAYS USE SHARP BLADES. BLUNT BLADES CAN CAUSE THE KNIFE TO SLIP AND CUT YOU MORE EASILY.

JUNIOR HACKSAW
When sawing, keep the saw upright and cut on the push stroke using the whole length of the saw. You shouldn't need to push hard.

SERRATED BREAD KNIFE
For cutting foam pipe insulation on **Brontobot**, step 1. Beware of sharp edges!

BRADAWL
A hot bradawl is best for making round holes. If you don't have one, try using a Phillips screwdriver.

SCISSORS
Handy for cutting all sorts of materials, and stripping electrical wires. Take care with the sharp blades.

PLIERS
For twisting wires together in the Electra Extra section.

ELECTRICAL TAPE
Available at DIY stores. Useful for joining wires together in the Electra Extra section.

NIGHTLIGHTS
For heating up plastic and tools. See Heating Up Plastic panel.

CRAFT KNIFE
Great for cutting holes in plastic! See Hazard panel for safety tips on knives.

NO NEED TO USE A MONKEY WRENCH. JUST SIMPLE GADGETS AND A STURDY BENCH. REMEMBER TO FOLLOW THE GOLDEN RULES, AND YOU'LL BE SAFE WITH THESE HANDY TOOLS.

HEATING UP PLASTIC

BELOW ARE SAFETY HINTS FOR HEATING AND BENDING PLASTIC KNIVES, FORKS AND SPOONS USING A NIGHTLIGHT. **ALWAYS GET AN ADULT TO HELP YOU WITH THIS.**

● THE PLASTIC MAY GIVE OFF UNPLEASANT FUMES. WEAR A PAINT MASK TO PROTECT YOURSELF.

● TO AVOID UNNECESSARY FUMES, NEVER LEAVE THE PLASTIC OVER THE FLAME FOR LONGER THAN A FEW SECONDS.

● NEVER HOLD THE PLASTIC RIGHT IN THE FLAME AS IT WILL BURN AND GIVE OFF FUMES. HOLD IT AT LEAST 5CM AWAY FROM THE FLAME.

● KEEP FINGERS AWAY FROM THE FLAME AND THE AREA OF PLASTIC YOU INTEND TO HEAT.

● THICKER PIECES OF PLASTIC WILL TAKE LONGER TO HEAT UP THAN THINNER ONES.

● WHEN HEATING THE FORK ON **STEP 3 OF T-WRECKS** HOLD THE HANDLE ABOUT 5CM SPACING ABOVE THE FLAME WHEN HEATING IT, AND TWIST GRADUALLY.

● WHEN HEATING THE FORK PRONGS, HOLD THEM AT LEAST 7CM AWAY FROM THE FLAME. YOU MAY FIND THAT THEY BEND OVER BY THEMSELVES, BUT THEN BEND BACK THE OTHER WAY WHILST COOLING! TO AVOID THIS, DIP THE FORK IN A JAR OF COLD WATER STRAIGHT AWAY TO COOL THE PRONGS.

● REMEMBER, DIPPING HOT PLASTIC IN COLD WATER WILL IMMEDIATELY SET IT IN ITS NEW SHAPE AND WILL KEEP YOUR HANDS SAFE.

RUBBER GLOVES

Use for hot tool tasks, gluing and spray painting. All supermarkets sell them.

WIRE CUTTERS

You'll find these handy for snipping wires in the Electra Extra section. Great for cutting through wooden skewers, too!

SPRAY PAINT MASK

Available at any DIY store. You MUST wear one of these when you are spray-painting dinobots.

SPRAY PAINT

Great for applying large areas of colour. ALWAYS wear a spray paint mask when using spray paint! Comes in all colours!

ACRYLIC PAINT

Available in many colours from art shops. Ideal for painting plastic surfaces on dinobots. See Finishing Off, pages 10-11.

ARTISTS' PAINTBRUSHES

Buy these at any art shop in various sizes. Good for spot painting. See Finishing Off, pages 10-11.

SOLDERING IRON

Great for fixing wires in place. You MUST have adult help if you use them because they get very hot.

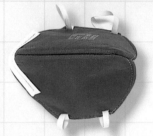

GLUE

A solvent-free contact adhesive is the best option. Always read the instructions on the packet. See the Hazard panel, too.

PHILLIPS SCREWDRIVER

Good for use on the Electra Extra section.

MARKER PEN

One which will write on plastic. You'll need this for drawing panels on dinobots. See Finishing Off, pages 10-11.

T-WRECKS

Tyrannosaurus Rex means King of the Tyrant Lizards. T-Wrecks means Tyrannical Wrecker and he'll rip you apart cog by cog in the battle zone. Massive jaws and claws do all the dirty work. This King of the Robovores can also inflict a lethal blow with one flick of his tail as he towers above everything else in the arena.

PARTS

- 8 plastic forks
- 1 wedge-shaped air freshener
- 1 trigger- action spray bottle
- 2 circular air fresheners
- 1 plastic coat hanger
- 2 metal bolts or screws
- 1 plastic drinking straw
- 3 wooden barbecue skewers
- 2 plastic wall plugs

YOU CAN ENERGISE T-WRECKS WITH SPINNING WHEELS AND MEAN GREEN EYES IN THE ELECTRA EXTRA SECTION.

! HAZARD

● IT IS IMPORTANT THAT YOU GET ADULT HELP FOR STEP 3, HEATING UP THE PLASTIC FORK. BEFORE ATTEMPTING THIS STEP, SEE THE 'HEATING UP PLASTIC' HAZARD PANEL ON THE TOOLS SPREAD (PAGES 6-7) FOR GUIDANCE AND SAFETY MEASURES.

● BE CAREFUL WHEN HEATING UP THE BRADAWL ON STEPS 1, 4, 7 AND 12. ASK FOR HELP AND WEAR KITCHEN GLOVES FOR SAFETY.

● BEWARE OF SHARP SCISSORS ON STEPS 8 AND 10.

● WHEN USING GLUE REMEMBER TO WORK IN A WELL-VENTILATED AREA AND TO KEEP IT AWAY FROM YOUR EYES.

TOOLS

- ● Spray paint mask
- ● Nightlight
- ● Junior hacksaw
- ● Wire cutters
- ● Bradawl
- ● Scissors
- ● Glue

HE'LL CRASH AND BASH AND CHAMP HIS JAWS THEN RIP YOU UP WITH TEETH AND CLAWS, SO SAY YOUR PRAYERS AND QUAKE WITH FEAR TYRANNOSAURUS WRECKS IS HERE!

ASSEMBLY

1 Using a heated bradawl, pierce axle holes through the spray bottle as shown. Make the front holes slightly higher than the back ones and just big enough to let the axles spin freely. Pull apart the circular air fresheners and discard the scented disks. Pierce holes in the centre of each half so that the axles fit tightly.

Trim to 1cm

Wooden skewer axle

Wall plug

Drinking straw

2 Assemble pairs of wheels with identical halves of the air fresheners. Use short lengths of drinking straw to space the wheels evenly from the body. Glue the wheels on to the axles. Snip off the excess to leave 1cm extending beyond the wheel. Glue a wall plug to each end.

3 Heat the neck (narrowest part) of a plastic fork over a nightlight and twist the handle through 90°. Gently heat the fork prongs and curl them downwards to make fierce claws. Prepare a second fork the same way.

4 Pierce a hole right through the neck of the spray bottle with a heated bradawl. A skewer should fit through easily, but not be too loose. Also pierce holes though the handles of the twisted forks and assemble the two arms on to the body by gluing them on to the skewer. Use small pieces of straw as spacers.

Pierced hole through handle of fork

5 Cut a rectangular hole in the back of the spray bottle for the tail to fit into.

6 Saw one arm from a coat hanger, including the centre section, and saw the metal hook off using your junior hacksaw.

7 Skewer

Tail should move up and down freely but not touch the ground

8 Take apart the wedge-shaped air freshener and snip out two or three of the ribbed pieces as shown.

9 Unscrew the top of the spray bottle, fit the air freshener lid over the neck (you may need to increase the size of the hole you cut in step 8) and screw down the top again.

Spray bottle top screws down on to air freshener lid

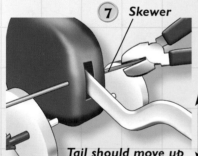

7 Pierce holes through the coat hanger centre and through the bottle on either side of the rectangular hole you cut. Assemble the tail using a skewer. Snip off the excess. If the tail does not move freely, cut the hole a little larger, above or below.

11 Glue three fork heads into either side of the wedge-shaped air freshener to form rows of vicious teeth.

12 Pierce a hole right through the air freshener head and the top of the spray bottle, using a heated bradawl, and insert a skewer through the hole. T-Wrecks can now open and close his jaws on the hinge you have made. If not, try the hole in a slightly different place. Snip off the skewer ends, and pierce holes just above the two ends for the screw eyes to fit into. With careful positioning, you should be able to hide the wooden skewer ends. Turn over for some finishing-off ideas and tips.

10 Heat up the remaining six plastic forks in a glass of warm water and cut off the handles.

Jaws should open and shut

FINISHING OFF

Adding paint effects to your dinobots is great fun and gives them that individual look. Here are some hints for special techniques that you can try. Combine them with the brilliant stickers provided for a stunning finish.

Getting a smooth, overall metallic look is best achieved using spray paints, but you can also buy brush-on metallic paints in 'safe-to-use' acrylics. Either way your robots will be able to do battle like knights in shining armour-plating.

TOP TIPS

● HANG DINOBOTS ON A WASHING LINE TO SPRAY THEM. THAT WAY YOU CAN SPRAY FROM ALL ANGLES AND WON'T GET SPRAY ON FLOORS OR OTHER SURFACES.

● SHAKE WELL AND KEEP THE SPRAY CAN MOVING. SPRAYING TOO LONG IN ONE SPOT WILL CAUSE RUNS.

● SEVERAL THIN COATS ARE MUCH BETTER THAN ONE THICK COAT OF PAINT.

● CHECK OUT THE WIDE RANGE OF METALLIC COLOURS AT YOUR LOCAL MOTOR OR HARDWARE STORE. THERE ARE EVEN GLITTER PAINTS AND HIGH-SHEEN CHROME SPRAYS AVAILABLE.

● ON RAINY DAYS, USE A LARGE CARDBOARD BOX AS A SPRAY BOOTH IN THE GARAGE.

TOOLS

- ● Spray paints
- ● Pots of bright colours
- ● Spray paint mask
- ● Rubber gloves
- ● Brushes
- ● Permanent marker pens
- ● Overalls or worn-out old clothes

SPRAY CANS. MARKERS. PAINT BRUSH TOO. CHOOSE YOUR STICKERS. IT'S UP TO YOU!

HAZARD

● WEAR A PAINT MASK WHEN USING AEROSOL CANS TO AVOID INHALING PAINT FUMES.

● WHEN USING SPRAY PAINTS, ALWAYS MAKE SURE YOU ARE IN A WELL-VENTILATED AREA (e.g. OUTSIDE).

● ALWAYS READ THE INSTRUCTIONS ON CANS OF SPRAY PAINT.

● PROTECT YOUR HANDS AND CLOTHES WITH RUBBER GLOVES AND AN OVERALL. IF YOU HAVEN'T GOT AN OVERALL, WEAR SOME WORN-OUT OLD CLOTHES. THEN IF YOU GET A LOT OF PAINT ON THEM YOU CAN JUST THROW THEM AWAY!

As well as the basic metallic finish described in Top Tips, try some of the following or invent your own.

Use lighter colours first, allow to dry, then add darker colours

Spitfire-style camo patches

SPOT PAINTING

Add bright areas of paint using acrylic model paints. These should be used straight from the pot. Always start with lighter colours and go over them with darker colours when the first coat has dried. Brontobot looks pretty fierce with a yellow and red flame effect. Wash your brushes well between colours.

CAMOUFLAGE

Some dinobots prefer the advantage of camouflage. Use green or brown colours to paint Spitfire-style camo patches. You could draw the patches on with a soft pencil first, before painting them in.

DRY BRUSHING

Use a piece of kitchen roll to clean off most of the paint from your brush, then dust the brush lightly over your dinobot to give it a tarnished, or rusty, effect. Black and orange are the best colours for this. Dusting over any ridges and edges with paint will make all the details stand out clearly.

Tarnished rusty effect

Kitchen roll

PANELS

Painting fine lines with a brush is very difficult. Use a permanent marker pen instead and draw on panels and rivets to give your dinobots that authentic robot look.

STRIPES

Even fierce predators use camouflage in the wild, like these black and orange tiger stripes. You could also try painting a green reptile scale effect, cracked elephant skin texture or tortoiseshell patterns. Nature books are a good place to look for inspiration.

ADDING STICKERS

Each dinobot has its own set of special stickers. There are also lots of other logos and details on the sheet for you to add after painting. Try to make your robots look symmetrical by adding the same markings to each side. You can also make your own stickers by cutting logos and patterns from magazines and gluing them with contact adhesive.

Studs sticker fits in top of head

Panels on head

Crash test spiral sticker

Skull and cross-bones stickers show how many battles won in Arena

Spot-painted flames around mouth

Crash test stickers on claws

Dry brushing on forearms and claws

Official Dinosaur Robots badge sticker

Tiger stripes on neck

Scratch-mark sticker on neck

Chevron stickers on tail

Camouflage on body, tail and wheels

T-Wrecks specially designed sticker

TERROR-SAW

This dinobot may not be able to soar like its reptilian ancestors, but it sure can fly off the handle when provoked. Outstretched wings can inflict glancing blows on the enemy, and it spins with elegance on those razor-thin wheels to introduce a multi-fanged buzz-saw blade into the fray.

HOW ABOUT MOTORISING THAT TERRIBLE BUZZ SAW OF HIS IN THE *ELECTRA EXTRA* SECTION?

PARTS

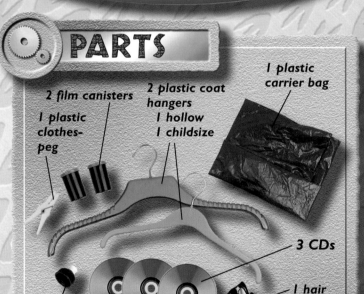

- 2 film canisters
- 1 plastic clothes-peg
- 2 plastic coat hangers
  - 1 hollow
  - 1 childsize
- 1 plastic carrier bag
- 3 CDs
- 1 hair gripper
- 1 pop-up drink bottle cap
- 1 wooden skewer

TOOLS

- Junior hacksaw
- Bradawl
- Wire cutters
- Scissors
- Glue
- Spray paint mask

HAZARD

- BE CAREFUL WHEN USING THE HOT BRADAWL ON STEP 3, AND SHARP SCISSORS ON STEPS 6 AND 8.
- BEWARE OF SHARP EDGES WHEN CUTTING UP THE CD ON STEP 8. ALTERNATIVELY FOR THE SAW BLADE, YOU COULD USE A CIRCLE OF CARD (ABOUT 12CM IN DIAMETER). THIS MAY BE A LESS HAZARDOUS OPTION?
- NEVER GET GLUE TOO NEAR TO YOUR EYES.

BEWARE OF THE ROBOT *PTERODON* WHO CHEWS UP OTHER 'BOTS FOR FUN. WITH BAT-LIKE WINGS AND RAZOR BILL THAT 'TERROR-SAW' OF HIS CAN KILL.

1 Saw about 6cm from the end of the hollow coat hanger using your hacksaw. (Terror-Saw's head will go on to the cut end.) Saw off the metal hook.

6cm

2 Remove the lids of the two film canisters and glue them to the centre of each CD. (Make sure that the outside of the canister top is glued to the printed side of the CD.)

3 Using a heated bradawl, pierce holes through the centre of the coat hanger, so that a skewer fits easily, and through the centres of the canister bottoms and tops, so that a skewer fits tightly.

4 Push the film canister tops and CDs on to the canisters themselves then assemble the wheels by pushing a skewer right through the wheels and coat hanger. If you made all your holes the right size you won't need any glue or spacers to keep the wheels and body apart, just leave a slight gap between the canisters and the coat hanger.

Wire cutters

Leave a slight gap between the canisters and the coat hanger.

5 Saw the metal hook from the smaller, solid coat hanger and glue a piece of plastic carrier bag on to one side of the hanger.

6 When dry, trim the excess plastic from the coat hanger and cut a wavy pattern to form the wings.

7 Open out the hair gripper and glue it into the shorter side of the hollow coat hanger body, just above the wheels. The teeth of the gripper make a very convincing rib cage and hold the wings firmly in place. Glue the wings into the highest pair of teeth in the gripper. (See Top Tips on page 5 about hair grippers.)

Wings glue into gripper

8 Cut a saw-tooth pattern in the third CD with strong scissors. Heating your CD in hot water first will prevent it from shattering when cut.

Pop-up cap secures CD on to bottle top

CD fits on to bottle top

9 Prise the pop-up cap from the bottle top and assemble the saw by placing the CD on to the top and replacing the pop-up cap. This will take some force. Glue the saw assembly to the end of Terror-Saw's tail (which is the uncut end of his coat hanger body). Do this after spray painting your finished robot if you want to keep your CD shiny.

Plastic clothes-peg with one arm cut off makes head

FINISHING

10 Cut one arm from a plastic clothes-peg to make the head and glue it in place on the neck. Then spray Terror-Saw with some terror-coloured paint, add some terror-stickers and prepare for battle!

Add Terror-Saw's specially designed stickers as shown

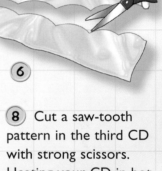

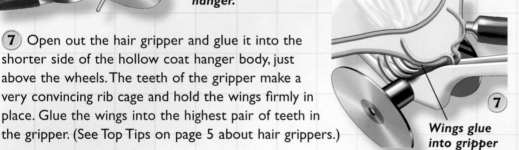

CYBER-CERATOPS

The art of robot battling is to attack and defend at the same time. This beast can do exactly that. With the horns of a Triceratops and the armoured-plates of a Stegosaurus, you get the best of both species. Though Cyber isn't limited to three horns, this horned headbutter is a true Septa-ceratops. With a sideways swipe of its tail there's also the added feature of a double-edged grass cutter to cut the enemy down to size.

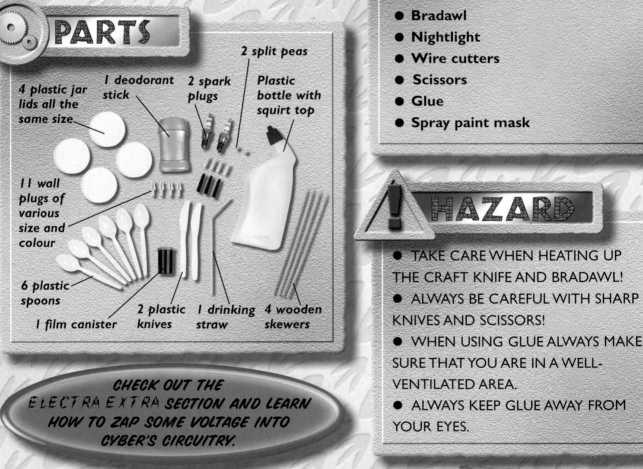

PARTS

- 4 plastic jar lids all the same size
- 1 deodorant stick
- 2 spark plugs
- 2 split peas
- Plastic bottle with squirt top
- 11 wall plugs of various size and colour
- 6 plastic spoons
- 1 film canister
- 2 plastic knives
- 1 drinking straw
- 4 wooden skewers

TOOLS

- Craft knife
- Bradawl
- Nightlight
- Wire cutters
- Scissors
- Glue
- Spray paint mask

HAZARD

- TAKE CARE WHEN HEATING UP THE CRAFT KNIFE AND BRADAWL!
- ALWAYS BE CAREFUL WITH SHARP KNIVES AND SCISSORS!
- WHEN USING GLUE ALWAYS MAKE SURE THAT YOU ARE IN A WELL-VENTILATED AREA.
- ALWAYS KEEP GLUE AWAY FROM YOUR EYES.

CHECK OUT THE ELECTRA EXTRA SECTION AND LEARN HOW TO ZAP SOME VOLTAGE INTO CYBER'S CIRCUITRY.

THOSE ARMOUR-PLATES AND HORNS OF STEEL
SURE MAKE THE OPPOSITION SQUEAL,
WITH CYBER-CERATOPS AROUND
THE SAFEST PLACE IS UNDERGROUND!

ASSEMBLY

1 Using a heated craft knife, cut slots in the film canister as shown. There should be four slots in all, positioned so that the two plastic knives fit tightly at about a 30° angle to each other. (See step 2.)

Pierced hole

Pierced hole

Wooden skewer goes right through bottle and canister

4 Pierce holes in the plastic bottle as shown, so you can fit the tail in place using a wooden skewer pushed right through the holes in the bottle and film canister. This may be a bit tricky if the knives move out of line. If you can't keep the holes lined up, try gluing the knives in place beforehand.

8 Pierce a hole through the top of the bottle using your heated bradawl and push the head assembly in place after snipping the skewer off to the right length, (about 4cm).

Head fits into hole in bottle top

2 Push the plastic knives in place with the saw edges facing outwards. Using a heated bradawl, pierce a hole right down through the centre of the film canister assembly. A wooden skewer should fit quite freely through the holes.

Pierce holes in film canister top and bottom

5 Using a heated bradawl, pierce holes through the centre of each plastic jar lid, and through the bottle, for axle holes. Measure carefully from the back or front of the bottle to make sure the holes line up. Assemble the wheels using short lengths of plastic straw as spacers, and wall plugs as deadly wheel spikes. Glue the wheels and plugs in place but make sure the axles spin freely in the robot body itself.

centre hole

6 Pierce a hole right through the centre of the empty deodorant stick, for the neck to fit through, and holes at the front and back of the head for locating Cyber's horns.

9 Warm up the six plastic spoons in hot water and snip off the handles with scissors, keeping one for step 10.

FINISHING

11 Glue the armoured-plate assembly in place on the back of Cyber-Ceratops and cut a hole in each side of the body for a spark plug to screw into. The hole need not be round (a tricky job with a craft knife) but can be square. The spark plug should screw in tightly.

Hole spark plug screws into

3 Cut a rectangular slot in the bottom of the plastic bottle which is just big enough for the film canister assembly to fit through.

Straw spacers

Wooden skewer

Wall plugs on axles

7 Glue wooden skewers in each of the horn holes and a longer skewer through the central hole. Two split peas, glued in place, will form the eyes.

Split peas (eyes)

Longer skewer

Wall plugs glued on to skewers (horns), front and back

10 Glue the spoons on to the handle as shown and glue each spoon to the back of its opposite.

Point where each spoon rests on the back of its opposite

Neck

Add Cyber-Ceratops specially designed stickers as shown

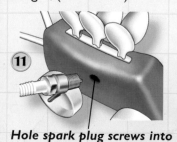

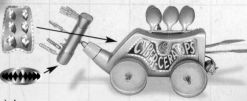

BRONTOBOT

ADULT HELP RECOMMENDED

Sturdy, spiny, steerable, and unstoppable. That's what you get when you sign up for Brontobot. He can smash just about anything in his path with his battering-ram head and, with fully manoeuvrable wheels, that path can lead anywhere. Anyone who cares to sneak up from behind had better beware, too. With his club tail of spikes, this dinobot can fend off attackers from all directions.

PARTS

- 3 wooden skewers
- 8 bottle caps
- 1 piece of garden hose
- 1 plastic drinking straw
- 1 plastic bottle with a swan-shaped neck
- 1 ping-pong ball
- 4 wall plugs
- Split peas
- 1 side of a circular air freshener
- 1 piece of pipe insulation foam
- 1 plastic coat hanger
- 1 fabric softener lid

TOOLS

- Craft knife
- Serrated bread knife
- Bradawl
- Wire cutters
- Glue
- Junior hacksaw
- Nightlight
- Spray paint mask

HAZARD

- WATCH OUT FOR THE SHARP EDGE OF THE SERRATED KNIFE ON STEP 1. YOU MAY WANT AN ADULT TO HELP YOU.
- WHEN USING GLUE, MAKE SURE YOU ARE IN A WELL-VENTILATED AREA AND KEEP GLUE AWAY FROM YOUR EYES.
- ALWAYS BE CAREFUL WHEN USING A HEATED BRADAWL..
- REMEMBER TO KEEP YOUR FINGERS CLEAR OF THE HACKSAW BLADE WHEN SAWING ON STEP 8.
- TAKE CARE WHEN USING THE SHARP CRAFT KNIFE ON STEP 9.

IN THE ELECTRA EXTRA SECTION YOU WILL FIND OUT HOW TO GET BRONTOBOT BUZZING ON BATTERY POWER.

A HEAD THAT'S THICK AND BUILT TO RAM, A TAIL WITH PIERCING SPIKES THAT SLAM, THIS METAL MONSTER'S GOT THE LOT. OF COURSE WE'RE TALKING BRONTOBOT!

1 Using a serrated bread knife, cut four wheels from the foam pipe insulation. The two front wheels should be about 3cm thick and the rear wheels about 5cm thick.

5cm

3cm

1

4

2 Glue the eight bottle caps to the centres of each wheel. Pierce holes through the wheels so that a wooden skewer fits tightly.

2

Pierced holes

3

Neck points up

3 Assemble the rear wheels by piercing a hole near the back of the bottle with a heated bradawl and pushing a skewer right through the wheels and body. Check the axle spins freely. If not, make the hole bigger before fitting the second rear wheel. Snip the ends off the skewer with sharp scissors or wire cutters.

Thin triangle snipped in pipe

6

4 Use the side of the circular air freshener as a steering wheel. Pierce a hole through its centre, through the neck of the bottle and through the ping-pong ball. A skewer should fit tightly through the wheel and ball but loosely through the bottle. Assemble the steering mechanism as shown.

5 Pierce another pair of holes through the ping-pong ball at right angles to the first holes. This time a skewer should fit loosely. Assemble the front axle and wheels as shown. Snip off the excess skewer.

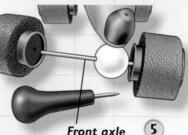

Front axle **5**

6 Depending on the size of your garden hose, force one end over the bottle neck after removing the screw cap – or push it inside the bottle neck (whichever is easiest). You can help it to fit inside by snipping a thin triangle out of the end of the hose to allow it to compress.

7 Pierce a hole through the other end of the hose pipe and through the fabric softener lid. Join them together using a small piece of skewer. Brontobot's head can now move from side to side to vary the angle of his battering ram capability. Glue on split peas for eyes.

Split pea

7

Skewer

8 Saw the metal hook from the coat hanger and saw off one of the arms.

8

9 Cut a slot in the back of Brontobot's body for the tail to fit through. This should extend down the back edge about 4cm and up across the top edge the same distance.

4cm

9

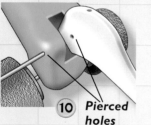

10 *Pierced holes*

10 Pierce holes through the wide end of the tail and through the body of the robot on either side of the slot you cut. Push a wooden skewer through the hole to form a hinged tail. Test the tail to make sure it can be raised and dropped to pound the enemy from behind.

11 Pierce holes at right angles through the end of the tail. Push small pieces of skewer though the holes and glue wall plugs on to each protruding stick.

11

12

Coat hanger

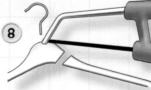

12 Glue a straight piece of coat hanger, from the arm you cut off earlier, across the back of Brontobot as a spine. Glue rows of split peas beside the spine to give a tough, rivetted effect.

Split peas

Position Brontobot's specially designed sticker as shown

BALLISTASAURUS

With the crested head of Parasaurolophus and the body of a container of motor oil, this dinobot almost runs on fossil-fuel. Its weapon is a powerful catapult (ballista) which can be loaded with marbles, dried peas or lumps of modelling clay. A single roller out front is mounted on an adjustable pair of arms so Ballistasaurus can arch upwards and increase his range of fire. Opponents would do well to stay out of it!

PARTS

3 screws

1 tall screw cap

1 spray bottle head with the pipe attached

2 coat hangers (1 hollow)

1 plastic clothes peg

3 wooden skewers

1 plastic clothes peg

2 small bottle caps

1 drinking straw

2 large plastic lids

1 large motor oil bottle

2 spray can lids of different sizes

TOOLS

- Craft knife
- Screwdriver
- Bradawl
- Wire cutters
- Glue
- Junior hacksaw
- Nightlight
- Spray paint mask

CHARGE UP BALLISTA IN THE *ELECTRA EXTRA* SECTION AND GET HIM CHARGING INTO BATTLE LIKE A BOLT OF LIGHTNING!

HAZARD

- WHEN USING GLUE, MAKE SURE YOU ARE IN A WELL-VENTILATED AREA AND KEEP GLUE AWAY FROM YOUR EYES.
- ALWAYS BE CAREFUL WHEN USING A HEATED BRADAWL.
- REMEMBER TO KEEP YOUR FINGERS CLEAR OF THE HACKSAW BLADE WHEN SAWING ON STEPS 3 AND 8.
- TAKE CARE WHEN USING THE SHARP CRAFT KNIFE ON STEP 9.

WHEN BALLISTASAURUS TAKES A SHOT HIS CATAPULT CAN HIT THE SPOT. SO RUN AND HIDE, AND DUCK YOUR HEAD THIS DINOBOT IS ONE TO DREAD

ASSEMBLY

1 Glue the two smaller bottle caps to the centre of the larger plastic lids. Pierce holes right through each wheel so that a skewer fits tightly.

Pierced holes

①

4cm straw spacers **②**

② Use a heated bradawl to pierce a hole through the motor oil bottle, large enough for a wooden skewer to fit through easily. Assemble the wheels and axle on to the robot body. Use 4cm spacers cut from a plastic drinking straw to stop the wheels rubbing against the bottle. Snip off the excess skewer.

3 Saw the two arms from a hollow coat hanger, as shown, using a junior hacksaw.

③ **③**

Pierced hole through oil bottle

⑥

Cap rests on second skewer

4 Pierce holes through the coat hanger arms at each end, and at a distance of about 3cm from the cut end, as shown. A wooden skewer should fit tightly through these holes. Also pierce holes through the centre of the two spray can lids so that a skewer fits loosely.

Pierced holes

④

Spray can lid wheel assembly

Second skewer

⑤

6 Pierce a hole right through the oil bottle just behind the screw cap and make sure it is large enough for a skewer to fit through easily. Now join the wheel mechanism on to the body of Ballista using a skewer, which can then be trimmed to size. The screw cap should rest on the second skewer to prevent it from touching the ground. Ballistasaurus can now arch himself up and bend in the middle to adjust his angle of fire.

5 Assemble the wheel and arms by slotting the smaller spray can lid inside the larger one (no need for glue) and passing a skewer through the whole wheel assembly. Fit a second skewer through the next set of holes, glue it in place and trim to the right length.

7 Pierce a hole through the screw cap as shown and insert the plastic spray bottle head using the pipe already attached. Snip the pipe off just below the screw cap. Glue half of the plastic clothes-peg to the top of the head for a horn and pierce eye holes in either side of the head into which you can screw two bolts or metal screws.

Half a plastic clothes peg

⑦

Pierced hole through screw cap

8 Saw the metal hook and one arm from the other coat hanger using your junior hacksaw.

⑧

9 Cut a slot in the rear of the bottle, large enough for the hanger to fit into. The slot should extend up and over the top of the bottle slightly.

⑨

10 Pierce holes in the bottle on either side of the slot and also through the central part of the coat hanger tail. Hinge the tail to the bottle using a wooden skewer then snip off the excess. If the tail doesn't swing right up, cut the slot larger.

⑩

Pierced holes in bottle

11 Pierce a hole down into the end of the tail using a heated bradawl.

⑪

FINISHING

12 Make a hole in the tall screw cap and fix the cap securely in place on the end of the tail as a catapult cage, using a long screw.

⑫

Cap screws on to tail

⑫

Position Ballistasaurus's specially designed stickers as shown

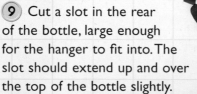

BATTLE BANK

Once you've built your Dinobot Warriors, you'll want to pit them against each other in battle and see who comes out on top. So read on to learn the art of Dinobot Duelling.

Whether you're controlling your robots with a motor and batteries or by hand, you'll need to know what they can and can't do. Practise steering, charging, turning, firing and chopping with tails, heads, saw blades and wheel spikes. Remember, a champion Dinobot Warrior combines skilfully built hardware and finely tuned skills in operating it. We're talking about survival of the fittest.

Damaging robots made from plastic junk is pretty hard unless you attack them with a jackhammer. You must simulate damage another way. The method below works well.

MESOZOIC CHALLENGE

Attach glass marbles or steel ball bearings to your robots using pieces of Blutak, modelling clay or bread dough. Each marble represents a life. When all the 'lives' have been knocked off it is officially 'extinct'.

Study the battle rules then draw up a list of contenders. Team up with friends (or enemies) who are willing to take part in your contests.

Breaking any of the battle rules incurs a penalty of one life. The opposition is allowed to remove a marble of their choice from the offending player's dinobot.

TEN RULES OF BATTLE

- Each player takes turns to carry out moves.
- Each player must energise his or her dinobot with six lives (marbles) prior to battle.
- The winner is the robot that knocks off all its opponent's marbles, or the one with the most marbles left after a timed battle.
- All marbles must be visible and accessible.
- No marble may be replaced once battle has commenced (even if they fall off on their own).
- Remove loose marbles from the arena at once.
- Game-play is paused whilst 'dead' marbles are removed from the arena.
- No player may tamper with or restick loose marbles once the contest is underway.
- Knocking off an opponent's marble entitles the player to an extra turn.
- Never attack a human operator.

In addition to these rules, the following three rules apply to non-motorised dinobot battles.
- No dinobot may be directly forced into an opponent. Attacks must be launched from a distance of at least 15cm.
- Dinobots may not be lifted off the ground in battle.
- Human operators may not touch an opponent's dinobot.

In either mode of battle, catapulting dinobots, like Ballistasaurus, may have unlimited numbers of missiles.

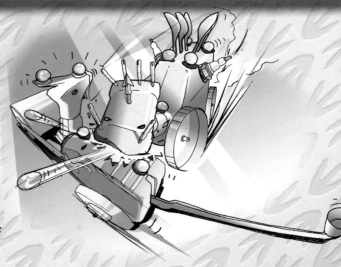

ARENA OF EXTINCTION

Arena floor area (1.5m x 1.5m)

5cm high barriers screwed to MDF arena floor

Ramps can be made by propping up flat pieces of wood or card on to wooden blocks

Brightly painted crates

Wedge blocks. These can make good ramps, too!

The inside and outside of your barriers can be decorated with chevron tape

Barrels painted in bright colours

Barriers can be made by taping pencils or dowel across two barrels

Battles should take place in a suitable arena. An official 'Arena of Extinction' is 1.5m square in size and should have a flat, even surface. Barriers to enclose the arena may be improvised using books or wood blocks. A more permanent arena may be constructed using a sheet of MDF (Medium Density Fibreboard) with 5cm high barriers, made from lengths of wood, screwed to the edges. Glue and screw the edge barriers in place, then paint the whole thing with poster paints. Check out the picture of the arena above for some other cool paint effects and layout ideas.

Extra blocks of wood can be sawn into the following shapes, painted and used as obstacles for more challenging battles.

Wedge blocks - Saw a length of wood into blocks then saw each block diagonally to make wedges.

Crates - Saw different kinds of cubes and cuboids from offcuts of wood.

Barrels - Saw lengths of round section wood, such as a broom handle.

A great way to obtain a whole collection of wood blocks is to ask at a local joiners' workshop for wood offcuts. They will be pleased to let you fill a carrier bag with all sorts of shapes and sizes (carpenter's junk).

Paint your obstacles with poster paints or cover them with stickers and labels.

For other Arena battle challenges, turn to page 22.

SHOW NO MERCY SPARE NO LIVES. IN THE BATTLE ARENA THE STRONGEST SURVIVES

PERMIAN CHALLENGE

Practise your skills by attaching marbles to the wooden obstacles you have made with Blutak or dough, then time how quickly you can knock them all off. Set a 3 minute egg-timer or stopwatch and try to knock off 12 marbles before your time runs out.

TRIASSIC CHALLENGE

Build a wall of wood blocks and see how easily you can demolish it. As with real battles, you must not force your dinobot into the wall. You may only launch it at the wall from a distance of not less than 15cm.

Instead of a wall of blocks, try demolishing a pyramid of barrels in as few moves as possible.

JURASSIC CHALLENGE

When practising on your own, you can still carry out a battle sequence by operating each dinobot in turn. You can keep switching sides and carrying out manoeuvres and attacks.

CRETACEOUS CHALLENGE

Add an extra element of chance to your battles, using dice. At the start of each turn, the player must throw a dice. The score will decide which moves you are permitted to make.

Score 1, 3 or 5 (odd numbers). This means you can move your dinobot around the arena, but not attack. If you make contact by accident you miss a turn next time around.

Score 2 or 4 (even numbers). This means you may move or attack, whichever you wish.

Score a 6. This entitles you to two turns in a row. On either turn you may move or attack the opponent.

SCORE SHEET

MESOZOIC CHALLENGE	PERMIAN CHALLENGE	TRIASSIC CHALLENGE	JURASSIC CHALLENGE	CRETACEOUS CHALLENGE

SCORING

Use the above scoresheet to record how well each dinobot does in each of the five challenges laid out in this book. You can devise ways of scoring for yourselves or, for example, you could write down how many marbles are left intact on each dinobot's body after a timed version of the Mesozoic Challenge. The dinobot with the most marbles left, wins. Or you can write down how many marbles are left on obstacles after each dinobot has completed the Permian challenge. This time the dinobot with the least number of marbles left is the winner! If you want to use this score sheet more than once, take photocopies for future games before you fill it in, or use a pencil?

ELECTRA EXTRA

Here we discover how to bring your dinobots to life with motors, lights and buzzers. Any of them can be battery powered and only a few tools are needed to do the job properly. I'll demonstrate using Cyber-Ceratops, but you can adapt the step-by-step instructions to suit Brontobot, T-Wrecks and Ballistasaurus. Terror-Saw has his own way of getting around. Power-up that saw blade, and you'll make him scuttle around like a beetle in a bathtub. Once a robot is fitted with its electrical components you'll need to build the simple remote control unit described in the following section. All the parts can be found in a hobby shop or electrical components store. Check that your motors and diodes are rated at the correct voltage and ask an adult to help with any soldering. Read the Hazard warnings carefully and always put safety first.

PARTS

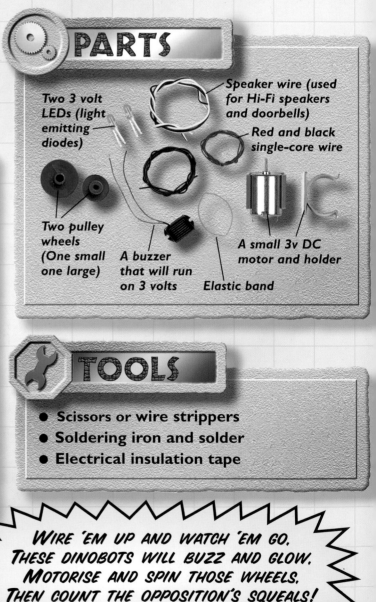

Two 3 volt LEDs (light emitting diodes)

Speaker wire (used for Hi-Fi speakers and doorbells)

Red and black single-core wire

Two pulley wheels (One small one large)

A buzzer that will run on 3 volts

Elastic band

A small 3v DC motor and holder

⚠ HAZARD

● YOU WILL NEED THE HELP OF AN ADULT TO SOLDER CONNECTIONS. THIS TOOL GETS VERY HOT AND CAN BURN. NEVER TRY TO USE ONE YOURSELF, UNLESS PROPERLY SUPERVISED.
● WHEN USING GLUE, MAKE SURE YOU ARE IN A WELL-VENTILATED AREA AND KEEP GLUE AWAY FROM YOUR EYES.
● BEWARE OF THE HOT END OF THE HEATED BRADAWL!
● WHEN STRIPPING WIRE, WATCH OUT FOR ANY STRAY WIRES WHICH MAY STICK INTO YOUR FINGERS. ALWAYS TRY TO KEEP STRIPPED WIRES TWISTED TOGETHER.

🔧 TOOLS

● Scissors or wire strippers
● Soldering iron and solder
● Electrical insulation tape

Wire 'em up and watch 'em go. These dinobots will buzz and glow. Motorise and spin those wheels. Then count the opposition's squeals!

Pierced hole **Bottle top**

Head

Body of robot

Front cover of Cyber-Ceratops head

1

1 Remove the head of Cyber-Ceratops and pull off the front cover (deodorant stick lid). Using a heated bradawl, pierce a hole close to the point where the skewer passes through the underside of the head. Now thread about 40cm of speaker wire right through the body of the robot, out through the neck, bottle top and head, so that the ends can be seen at the tail and front of the head.

LEDs fit into pierced eye holes

Buzzer

4

4 Pierce eye holes in the top of the head with a heated bradawl and glue the LEDs in place. Join both red wires from the diodes, the red wire from a buzzer and one speaker wire together. Soldering them will ensure a good connection. Join all black wires together and connect them to the other speaker wire.

7 Glue the motor holder to the back of Cyber-Ceratops, just below the tail. Fit a pulley wheel to the motor spindle and slot the motor into the holder. Attach an elastic band over both pulley wheels and solder the two speaker wires to the motor terminals. Once you've made the remote control unit (see pages 27-29), attach its own two speaker wires to the motor terminals using crocodile clips and you're ready to go.

Motor holder

Motor holder

7

Elastic band **Pulley wheel on motor spindle**

Remote control unit

2 Separate the speaker wires and strip the plastic coating from each wire at both the tail and the head ends.

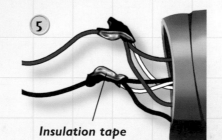

2

Plastic coating stripped from wires

5 Wrap insulating tape around all connections to stop them touching each other and causing a short circuit. Then push all the wires and buzzer into the head and replace the cover (deodorant lid). Refit Cyber's head back on to his shoulders.

5

Insulation tape

Longer diode leg (positive)

Shorter diode leg (negative)

3

3 Prepare four short lengths of wire, two red and two black. Twist and solder the red wires to the longer legs of the diodes (positive). Twist and solder the black wires to the shorter legs (negative).

Pulley wheel glued to wheel 6

6 Remove one of the rear wheels and glue a pulley wheel to the wheel itself. Replace the wheel and straw spacer then glue it securely to the axle.

TOP TIP

● Although the buzzer, LEDs and motor should be rated at 3 volts, you will need to use 6 volts to power them all at the same time. Two 1.5 volt batteries will not provide enough power when the wheels are being driven and the motor is drawing too much power for itself. If you do use just 3 volts your robot will run, but the LEDs will do little more than flicker on and off. Be sure to use a battery holder that takes four 1.5 volt batteries when you build the remote control unit. Normally, the 3 volt LEDs should not receive such a high voltage, but as long as you use them together with the buzzer and motor there will be little chance of damaging them.

MOTORISING TERROR-SAW'S SAWBLADE

(1)

Hole pierced right through tail mounting

Pulley wheel glued to under side of CD

TOP TIPS

● If you are fitting LED eyes to your robots and the eyes only glow when your robot is reversing, twist the elastic band on the motor pulley into a figure of eight. This will reverse the direction of wheel spin and give you the desired effect.
● Some modern LEDs will glow different colours depending on the direction of the current. Try them out – green for charging and red for retreating.
● You could try painting a spiral on the top side of your saw blade so that it creates an interesting effect when spinning.

(1) Remove the saw blade from Terror-Saw's tail. Glue a pulley wheel to the underside and fit a short piece of wooden skewer into the pulley wheel. Pierce a hole right through the tail mounting with a heated bradawl. This should be large enough to allow the skewer to fit through easily.

Pulley wheel fitted to motor spindle

Elastic band

Saw blade assembly mounted on tail

Remote control unit connected (see pages 27-29)

Motor holder with motor fitted into it

(2)

(2) Glue a motor holder to one side of Terror-Saw's body and fit a pulley wheel to the spindle. Fit the motor into its holder with the spindle facing upwards and stretch an elastic band around both pulley wheels. Once you have connected the remote control unit to the motor (see pages 27-29), Terror's saw will buzz into action. The vibration of the saw will also cause the whole robot to move around on a smooth surface all by itself. Unless you are including a buzzer and lights when you wire up Terror-Saw, 3 volts will be enough to power the saw blade, so build a remote with just two batteries attached to it.

REMOTE CONTROL UNIT

For those who wish to sit back and operate their dinobots from the safety of a comfy beanbag, check out this simple remote switch. It will provide all the power and functionality you need to start, stop, charge into battle or retreat to a safe corner for a moment's time-out. Check out the panels below before turning to page 28 to begin assembly.

TOOLS

- Bradawl
- Soldering iron and solder
- Scissors or wire strippers
- Either a small screwdriver or pliers (depending on your crocodile clips)

HAZARD

- THAT SOLDERING IRON CAN REALLY BURN! YOU MUST GET ADULT HELP IF YOU WANT TO USE ONE.
- WHEN USING GLUE, MAKE SURE YOU ARE IN A WELL-VENTILATED AREA AND KEEP GLUE AWAY FROM YOUR EYES.
- WATCH OUT FOR HEATED BRADAWL ON STEPS 2 AND 5.
- WHEN STRIPPING WIRE, WATCH OUT FOR ANY STRAY WIRES WHICH MAY STICK INTO YOUR FINGERS. ALWAYS TRY TO KEEP STRIPPED WIRES TWISTED TOGETHER.
- IF YOU ARE USING CROCODILE CLIPS WHICH PINCH TOGETHER BE CAREFUL, WHEN USING THE PLIERS TO CRIMP THEIR CONNECTING ENDS TOGETHER, NOT TO PINCH YOUR FINGERS!

PARTS

A 35mm film canister

A two-way switch

A battery holder that takes four AA batteries

About 1.5m of speaker wire

Red and black single-core wire

Two crocodile clips

Four AA batteries

A battery holder connector

START 'EM UP! FULL SPEED AHEAD, WITH THIS REMOTE THE FOE IS DEAD!

Switch has three positions; forwards, backwards and off

①

Pierced hole

Two wires of battery connector

②

Six pins with holes in

Two short wires with wire stripped from the end of each

① Study carefully the small two-way switch. It has three positions which can be used for forwards, backwards and off. The underside of the switch has six pins with small holes in them to connect your wires to. Although twisting the wires in these holes is possible, using a blob of solder will prevent them from working loose.

② Start by piercing a hole through the bottom of the 35mm film canister and pushing the two wires of a battery connector through it. Prepare two short wires, one black and one red, by stripping the plastic insulation from each end with wire strippers or scissors.

Battery connector wires twisted into holes in the pins

Two shorter wires connected from battery connector wire pins to two pins on the far side of switch

③

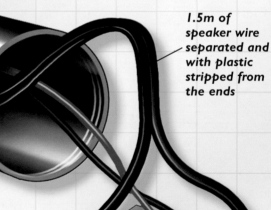

1.5m of speaker wire separated and with plastic stripped from the ends

④

Centre pins on switch

Connect two stripped ends of speaker wire to centre pins on switch

③ Twist a battery connector wire to each of the pins on one end of the switch. Connect the two short wires from these same two pins to the two pins on the far side of the switch, making sure that you cross them over as you do so. Solder all these connections to stop them from coming apart.

④ Take about 1.5m of speaker wire and push it through the hole in the bottom of the film canister. Separate the ends and strip the plastic from the wires. Now connect these two wires to the centre pins on the switch as shown and solder them in place. (See centre pins on the diagram on step 3.)

⑤ Pierce a hole through the lid of the film canister, large enough for the switch toggle to fit through. Secure the switch in the hole you have made with the washer and nuts provided. (Remember to remove them first, before the switch is pushed into the hole.)

Switch toggle fits into pierced hole in film canister lid, secured by washer and nuts provided

Battery connector clipped in place

Battery holder glued to side of film canister with connectors facing down

Secured lid on film canister with wire tucked inside

Four AA batteries in holder

⑥ Fit all the wires and switch into the film canister and securely push the lid in place. Glue a battery holder to the side of the film canister with the two connectors facing down and clip the battery connector to the holder. Install four new AA batteries into the holder once the glue has dried.

Green and red marks on this controller indicate forwards and backwards respectively

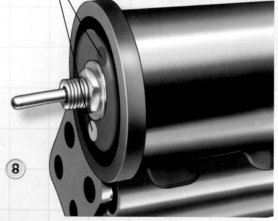

Other ends of speaker wires with wire stripped and crocodile clips connected

⑦ Strip the plastic from the other end of each speaker wire and connect a crocodile clip to the wires. These may have small screws or they may be the type that crimp together with pliers.

⑧ Paint a mark or put a sticker on the lid of your controller to show forwards and reverse. Remember, your remote controller is now set up to provide 6 volts of electricity to motors, LEDs and buzzers. If you are powering anything less than this, i.e. just a motor or LED lights on their own (with a typical rating of 3v), then you will need to use a battery holder that takes two AA batteries giving a total of 3 volts. Unless you do this you may damage the components you are using.

TOP TIP

● Wires can be twisted together tightly, but will probably work themselves loose unless soldered.

EVOLUTION

aking the five Dinobots as they are shown is the first step - helping them to evolve into new and exciting species is the next stage. You can add extra features, experiment with different shaped containers or combine all the best ideas you have discovered so far into one colossal MONSTERbot.

Use your imagination and unleash all that creativity designing battling dinos of your very own. There is a lot of fun and satisfaction to be had in the process.

Your local electronics store is a good place to discover ideas for Electra Extra projects. There are all sorts of buzzers, lights and special effects that can be incorporated into your designs.

WEBSITES

Here are some brilliant web addresses for you to visit as you go in search of the ultimate robot beast.

● **www.robosaurus.com**
The King of Metal-ivores. There are even videos of Robosaurus in action for you to download.

● **www.robotwars.co.uk**
The BBC Robot Wars official site.

● **www.battlebots.com**
Comedy Central's official Battlebots site.

● **www.ai.mit.edu/people/chunks**
Video footage and lots of images of a real experimental robot dinosaur called Troody at the Massachusetts Institute of Technology.

● **www.tekno-robot.com/dino.html**
See Rex and Steg, two toy fighting dinosaurs.

● **www.robotcombat.com**
The latest news and events in the world of robot battling.

● **www.machinebrain.com**
Lots and lots of links to other robot websites.

DESIGN TOP TIPS

● Keep a box handy in the garage or shed and ask the family to recycle containers and parts for you. Soon you'll have a treasure trove to dip into when it comes to new designs.
● Put together a scrapbook of pictures and ideas for robot building. You could cut them from magazines or print off pictures from the internet.
● Visit your local library and check out books on dinosaurs and robots for inspiration, then make drawings and sketches, just like a real designer.

DON'T GET LEFT BEHIND THE TIMES
DON'T BECOME A FOSSIL,
DESIGN A BREED OF ALL-NEW BOTS
FOR A GREAT JURASSIC JOSTLE!

GLOSSARY

Acrylic paint – resin-based paint that can be diluted with water.

Bradawl – a small, sharp-pointed tool for pushing holes through wood or plastic.

CD – Compact Disc

Crocodile clips – small metal clips with teeth that can be used to join wires together.

Diameter – the distance from one edge of a circle to the other, across the centre.

Electrical clips – small, plastic clips with a small nail in them, used to fix wires and cables to walls.

Electrical motor (3v DC) – a small machine that runs on battery power. The '**v**' stands for volts, and shows the strength of electrical current. **DC** stands for Direct Current, where the electricity flows in one direction from one pole of the battery to the other pole.

Electrical tape – also called insulation tape. Sticky, stretchy tape used for wrapping around bare wires to stop them from touching other wires and interfering with your circuit. As a safer alternative to soldering you can twist wires together firmly and cover the ends with small pieces of the tape.

LEDs – Light Emitting Diodes. Small electrical components that glow – usually green or red. These will only glow when the electricity is flowing in the right direction. You will have to experiment to find out which way works and which doesn't.

Manoeuvres – a series of movements requiring skill and care.

Mechanism – a set of moving parts that work together.

Mesozoic (Permian, Triassic, Jurassic and Cretaceous) – the names given to periods of time when dinosaurs walked the Earth.

Motorise – to add a motor.

Nightlight – a small, safety candle in a metal holder.

Phillips screwdriver – screwdriver with a narrow, star-shaped end rather than a wide, flat end.

Robovore – a robot that eats other robots.

Septa-ceratops – a seven-horned Ceratops which never actually existed. Tri-ceratops only had three horns.

Soldering – joining wires or metal surfaces using a soldering iron. The soldering iron is used to melt and apply the solder (a mixture of two or more metals) to the surfaces that need joining.

Tyrant – a cruel or oppressive leader.

Wall plugs – small, plastic parts for fixing screws into walls.

Wooden skewer – a long, thin piece of wood for holding food together in cooking.

First published in Great Britain in 2002 by The Chicken House, 2 Palmer Street, Frome, Somerset BA11 1DS Email chickenhouse@doublecluck.com
Text © Stephen Munzer 2002 Stephen Munzer has asserted his rights under the Copyright, Designs and Patents Act, 1988, to be identified as the author of this work. All rights reserved. No part of this publication may be reproduced or transmitted or utilised in any form or by any means, electronic, mechanical or otherwise, without prior permission of the Publisher.

Designed and produced exclusively for The Chicken House by Bean Bog Frag Book Design
Printed and bound by Leo Paper Products
ISBN 1 903434 75 0

Designers: Bean Bog Frag Book Design
Illustrators: Roger Goode, Will Barras, Stefan Chabluk
Photography by Chris R. Nottingham. Eye-Time Photgraphy

A CIP catalogue record for this book is available from the British Library

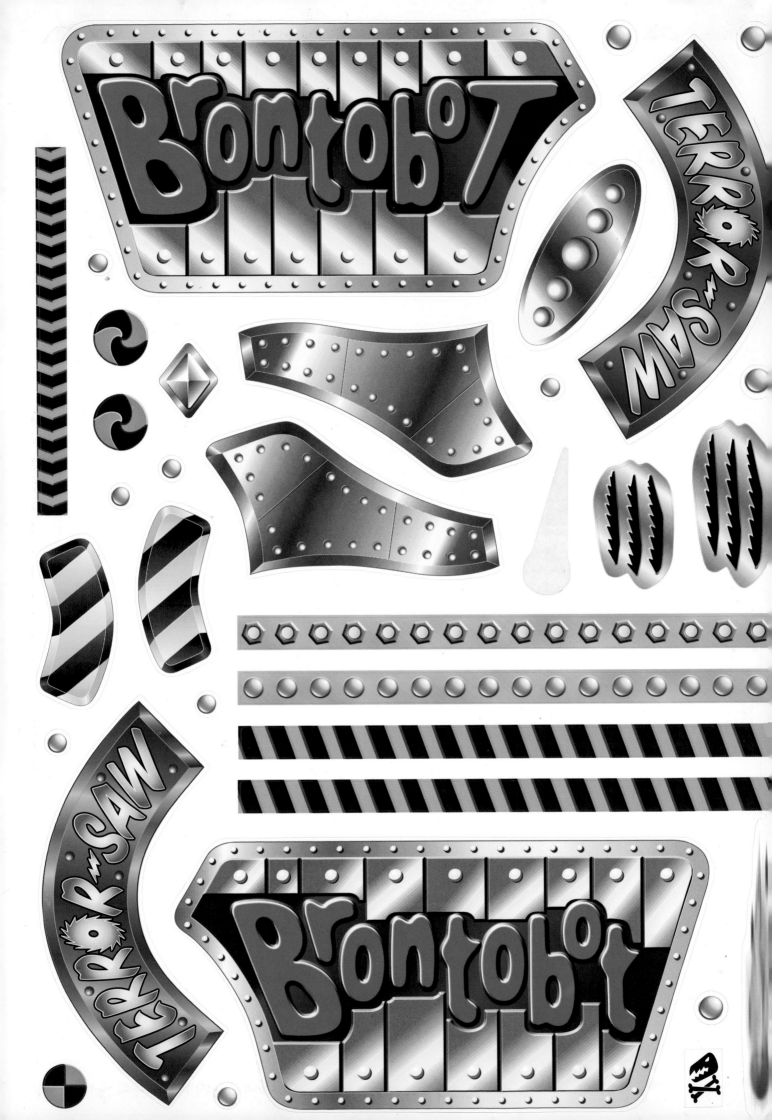

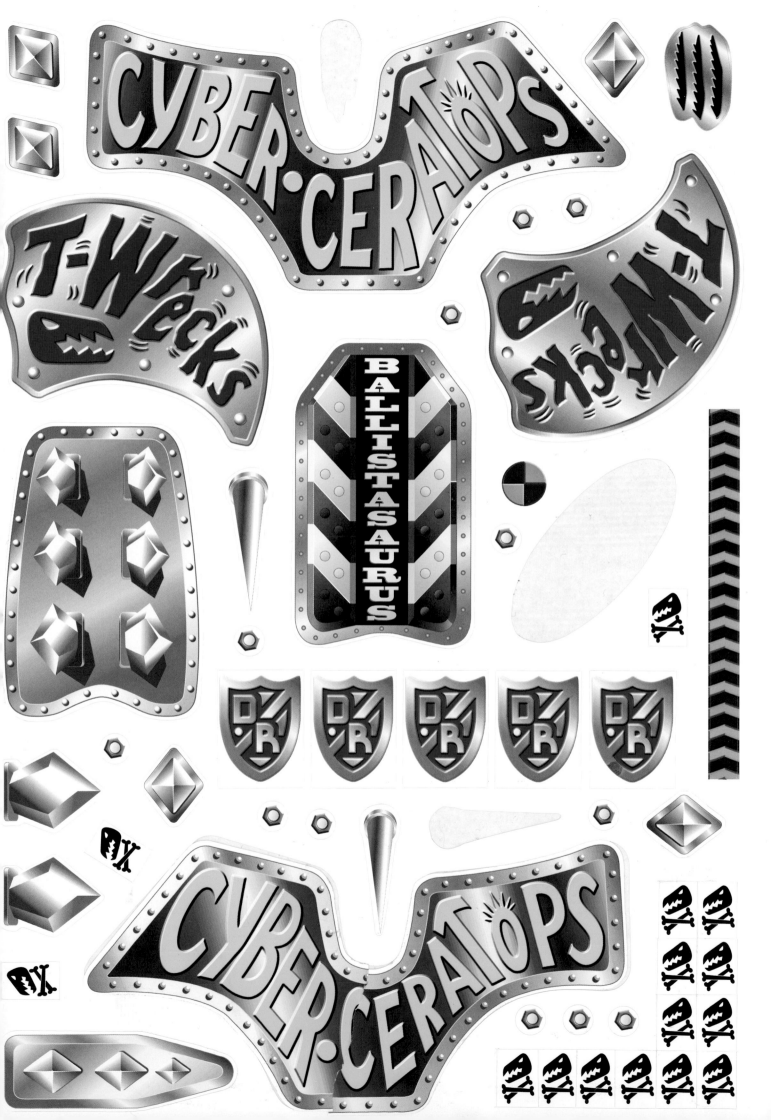